MARKET LE

Test File

INTERMEDIATE
BUSINESS ENGLISH

GW01326321

Christine Johnson

LTS Training and Consulting

Longman

FINANCIAL TIMES
World business newspaper.

Pearson Education Limited
Edinburgh Gate
Harlow
Essex CM20 2JE
England

First published 2000

ISBN 0 582 36572 4

Set in 10.5/12.5pt Meta Plus

Printed in Spain by Mateu Cromo, S.A. Pinto, Madrid

www.market-leader.net

Acknowledgements
We are indebted to the following for permission to reproduce copyright material:
Financial Times Limited for adapted extracts from 'Case Study: Ikea and Toys R Us' in FINANCIAL TIMES 8.10.97; 'Business school with a difference' in FINANCIAL TIMES 4.1.99; 'Foreign groups fuel ice cream wars in Vietnam' in FINANCIAL TIMES 5.1.99; 'Sales tumble at Korea groups' in FINANCIAL TIMES 5.1.99; article on Société Générale de Surveillance in FINANCIAL TIMES 5.1.99; article on Volkswagen in FINANCIAL TIMES 5.1.99; 'Xaar issues warning on full-year outcome' in FINANCIAL TIMES 5.1.99; 'Crossing the world from the township shebeens to the FTSE' in FINANCIAL TIMES 11.2.99; 'Daewoo and the art of customer focus' from MASTERING MARKETING SERIES PART 1 in FINANCIAL TIMES.

Designed by Jennifer Coles

Project Managed by Chris Hartley

Contents

Entry Test

Listening

You are going to hear a conversation between two colleagues. They are talking about moving to new offices.

You will hear the conversation twice.

1 Mark *all* the statements that are true.

  a) The first speaker (A) is happy about moving to a new office building.

  b) The second speaker (B) puts forward a different point of view.

  c) B was completely satisfied with the old office building.

  d) B thinks that they should talk to the management about their problem.

2 Which of the following advantages of the old office building are mentioned in the conversation?

  a) It is an attractive building.

  b) It is in a good location.

  c) It has lots of space for all the staff.

  d) It is easy to travel to work there.

  e) It has a good canteen.

  f) It is a modern building.

3 Which of the following advantages of the new office building are mentioned in the conversation?

  a) It is a modern building.

  b) It is easy to get there because there is a good bus service.

  c) It has more light.

  d) It is near the town centre.

  e) It has lots of space for all the staff.

  f) It is near good cafés and restaurants.

Vocabulary

A **Complete these sentences with the correct form of the word given in brackets.**

Example: The Finance .... *Manager* .... (manage) is in his office.

4 Our .... (compete) have brought out a new product and it looks very good.

5 After a long negotiation, we finally reached ....
(agree).

6 The Far East suffered from .... (economy) difficulties in the late 1990s.

7 The TZ4000 is our best-selling .... (produce).

8 The World Bank is an international .... (organise) that supports development projects around the world.

B **Match these words (9–18) with their definitions (a–j).**

9 advertisement   **a)** A reduction in the price offered by the seller.

10 customer   **b)** A person or company that makes goods from raw materials.

11 discount   **c)** What remains from a company's income from sales after its expenses have been deducted.

12 employer   **d)** An arrangement with a bank to borrow money with a promise to pay it back at a future date.

13 loan   **e)** A person or company who sells goods to you, usually on a regular basis.

14 manufacturer   **f)** A buyer, client or guest.

15 personnel   **g)** All the people who work for a company.

16 profit   **h)** A public notice selling goods or services.

17 research   **i)** A person or company who provides work for others.

18 supplier   **j)** Exploring a new market or developing a new product.

C **Make word partnerships between the verbs on the left and the nouns on the right.**

Example: write ———— a letter

19 lower   **a)** colleagues

20 make   **b)** a company

21 meet   **c)** the price

22 set up   **d)** a problem

23 solve   **e)** a profit

Grammar

A Write one word into each gap to complete this dialogue.

Example: Pleased to ......*meet*............... you.

Receptionist: Good afternoon. .... ²⁴ I help you?

John Dee: Good afternoon. My name is John Dee. I'm

.... ²⁵ Best Motors Ltd. I

.... ²⁶ an appointment with Mary Taylor at

2 o'clock.

Receptionist: Ah yes. Take a seat, please. Mrs Taylor

.... ²⁷ be with you in a moment, Mr Dee.

B Write a suitable phrase in each gap to complete this dialogue.

Example: **Ann:** How are you?

Michael: ....*I'm fine*...................., thanks.

Mrs Taylor: Good afternoon, Mr Dee. I'm Mary Taylor. Pleased to meet you.

John Dee: .... ²⁸, Mrs Taylor.

Mrs Taylor: Welcome to our company. .... ²⁹ a
good trip?

John Dee: Oh yes, it was fine thanks.

Mrs Taylor: .... ³⁰ a cup of coffee before we
start?

John Dee: Thanks very much, that would be nice.

Mrs Taylor: .... ³¹ milk and sugar?

John Dee: Just milk please.

C Choose the best word or phrase from the list below to complete the extract.

> John Dee .... ³² for Best Motors in the Sales Department. He
> .... ³³ with the company for three years now. He enjoys the job,
> although he spends .... ³⁴ time on the road visiting customers from
> all over Britain. Sometimes he travels hundreds of miles in a day. Last week, he
> .... ³⁵ more than 2,000 miles. If he .... ³⁶ make a long
> trip, he usually stays overnight in a hotel. His wife complains that he spends too
> .... ³⁷ time at home.

32 a) work	**b)** works	**c)** is working	**d)** is worked
33 a) is	**b)** was	**c)** has been	**d)** had been
34 a) many	**b)** a lot of	**c)** few	**d)** quite much
35 a) drive	**b)** drove	**c)** has driven	**d)** drived
36 a) would have to	**b)** will have to	**c)** had to	**d)** has to
37 a) little	**b)** few	**c)** short	**d)** less

D Choose the best word or phrase from the list to complete this e-mail message to John Dee from his department secretary.

> We have received some documents which .... ³⁸ to you. They are marked 'urgent'.
>
> When ....³⁹ back? Should I send ....⁴⁰ ?
>
> Sarah

38 a) address **b)** are addressed **c)** is addressed **d)** addressed
39 a) do you be **b)** you are coming **c)** you come **d)** will you be
40 a) them to you **b)** them you **c)** you **d)** to you them

E Choose the best word or phrase from the list to complete John's reply.

> Dear Sarah
>
> The documents are very important. ....⁴¹ please send them by courier?
>
> I ....⁴² at the Grange Hotel tonight and tomorrow, so they ....⁴³ there.
>
> Many thanks
>
> John

41 a) May you **b)** Shall you **c)** Could you **d)** Have you
42 a) stay **b)** am staying **c)** will staying **d)** am stay
43 a) deliver **b)** are delivered **c)** be delivered **d)** can be delivered

F Look at the bar chart and mark *all* the sentences which are both grammatically correct and describe the chart accurately.

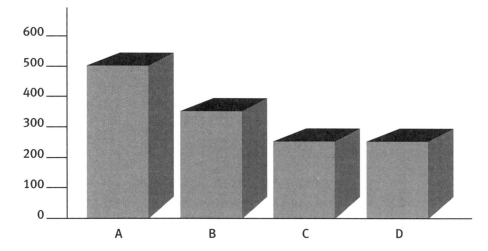

44 A had the highest sales.
45 Sales of C were lower as B.
46 Sales of D were the same like C.
47 B had higher sales than C or D.
48 Sales of A were twice as high as C.

Reading Read the text *Business School with a difference*. Some parts of the text have been taken out. These extracts are listed below the article. Complete each gap with the appropriate extract.

Business school with a difference

Every Wednesday evening for six weeks late last year, a group of young executives gathered in a small lecture room in New York. They sat in comfortable chairs ....⁴⁹. For three hours at a time, they tried to understand the difficult concepts which their professor talked about.

The sessions were intense, with the professor frequently stopping to call for questions or comments from individuals. Sometimes he asked for a show of hands on some problematic issues; ....⁵⁰.

What was unusual about the scene – apart from the quality of the technology and the lecture room – was that it was repeated simultaneously in 29 cities across the US. This meant that ....⁵¹.

The professor, ...⁵², is a member of the faculty at the University of Pennsylvania's Wharton School. The scheme is an ambitious attempt to offer a full Wharton executive education to ....⁵³, without reducing quality or damaging the school's brand.

One of the key advantages of the service is that it allows executives to keep up with the course even if they are moving around the country – ....⁵⁴.

Each professor, sitting in a room in Philadelphia, is surrounded by a group of eight teaching assistants. As participants around the country ask questions by sending a typed message, ...⁵⁵ who may answer them 'live' for the rest of the nation.

The session continues, with the aid of graphics on a board, and with ....⁵⁶. Students can read the notes from each three-hour session on a web site for the rest of the week.

At the end of the course, business plans that have been drawn up over the six weeks ....⁵⁷.

In New York, students seemed to enjoy the course, commenting that the variety of study methods helped them to participate and interact with professors and actually encouraged them to ....⁵⁸.

*Adapted from
the Financial Times*

---

a) can be physically submitted to Wharton professors for evaluation

b) with a computer console at each desk

c) 260 students were able to take each class at once

d) exhibits that appear on the screen at each student's desk

e) an advantage that conventional universities cannot match

f) become more involved than they did in real classes

g) at other times, the students formed groups to discuss a case

h) who appeared on a large screen

i) the assistants can either answer them directly, or pass them on to the professor

j) a mass audience

59 Mark *all* the following which are true.

a) At the Wharton School, the professors don't usually meet their students.

b) The professors can see their students during sessions.

c) The students attending these courses are people with no previous business experience.

d) Students cannot ask questions.

e) The students have home assignments to do as well as attending the sessions.

Progress Test 1 (Units 1–4)

Listening You are going to hear part of a speech given by Lorenzo Zambrano, Chief Executive of the Mexican company *Cemex*. At the time of this speech, *Cemex* was the world's third largest cement producer. (Cement is a material used in building.)

Mr Zambrano describes how and why his company became a global company. You have one minute to read the questions below before you listen. You will hear the speech twice.

1 Put the following events in the correct order according to when they happened. Start with the event which happened first. Write a letter on each line.

a) *Cemex* started expanding into Asia.

b) Mexico opened up its economy to foreign investors.

c) *Cemex* bought cement plants in Spain and South America.

d) There was a financial crisis in Mexico.

e) *Cemex* decided to become a global company.

f) *Cemex* acquired two companies in the US.

g) *Cemex* took over two other Mexican producers.

1st event: ....*b*..........

2nd event: ....

3rd event: ....

4th event: ....

5th event: ....

6th event: ....

7th event: ....

2 Complete these sentences with the figures or dates that were given.

a) *Cemex* decided to globalise in the mid ....

b) In the next ten years, *Cemex* increased production to .... tonnes.

c) *Cemex* invested over .... dollars in modernising its new plants.

d) During the economic crisis, income from the Mexican operations fell by ....%.

3 What were the reasons why *Cemex* decided to become a global company? Mark *all* those that Mr Zambrano mentions.

a) There was strong competition from large international companies.

b) *Cemex* was losing money.

c) It was difficult to expand further in Mexico.

d) To avoid being taken over by a bigger company.

Vocabulary

A To which industry does each of these companies belong? Match the descriptions (4–9) with the industries (a–f).

4 This company operates a chain of supermarkets.

5 This company provides power from nuclear power plants to other industries.

6 This company develops and sells drugs for a range of medical applications.

7 This company supplies cloth to clothing manufacturers.

8 This company manufactures such items as TVs, video recorders and CD players.

9 This company audits the finances of other companies and prepares their annual financial statements for them.

a) accountancy

b) consumer electronics

c) electricity generation

d) food retailing

e) pharmaceuticals

f) textiles

B Complete these sentences with an appropriate word.

Example: He didn't hear what the speaker said, so he asked her to

.... *repeat* .... what she had said.

10 Several passengers .... about the poor quality of food served on the flight.

11 The market research team has carried out a .... to test product awareness.

12 If you always buy the same brand, you are said to be .... to that brand.

13 When a number of companies agree to work together on a large project, such as a building, a bridge or a tunnel, we say that they form a ....

14 Radio, TV and newspapers are examples of ....

C Choose the best word to complete these sentences.

15 We are planning a mailshot to .... our new product.
 a) enter   b) launch   c) endorse   d) target

16 The advertising campaign will .... younger consumers.
 a) target   b) promote   c) persuade   d) access

17 This watch is not a genuine Rolex. It is a ....
 a) fraud   b) counterfeit   c) copycat   d) corruption

18 When you travel by plane, you can choose to sit by the window or in a(n) .... seat.
 a) corridor   b) passage   c) aisle   d) outside

D The following adjectives describe an unsuccessful product. Change them to their opposites: adjectives that describe a successful product.

Example: dull   ....*exciting*...................

19 poor quality   ....

20 overpriced   ....

21 badly made   ....

22 unknown   ....

23 old-fashioned   ....

Grammar

A Complete this report by writing the correct form of the verbs given in brackets. Use either the past simple or the present perfect.

Example: He ....*answered*.......... (answer) the telephone and gave his name.

Report on meeting about advertising strategy

In a meeting held last Monday, the Marketing Department proposed that the company should change its advertising strategy. It ....[24] (be) the policy in the past to use TV as the main medium for advertising our products. However, in the last year, there ....[25] (be) a number of changes. The cost of TV advertising ....[26] (rise) considerably since the beginning of last year. For example, whereas a one-minute prime-time slot ....[27] (cost) £500,000 last year, it now costs £750,000. In addition, the results of our TV advertising campaign last year ....[28] (be) very disappointing. Market research, which we ....[29] (conduct) between October and December last year, ...[30] (show) only a slight increase in sales following the campaign. On the other hand, sales resulting from our radio advertising campaign ....[31] (increase) substantially since last October. This is probably because we ....[32] (target) a younger audience through our radio campaign by linking advertising to pop music programmes. What is more, the cost of radio advertising ....[33] (not, increase) as much as TV advertising over the last year. Our conclusion is that TV advertising should be cut in favour of greater emphasis on radio.

B Study the chart comparing three models of electronic notebook. Then complete the sentences. Write *one* word in each gap.

	Model A	Model B	Model C
Weight	180 g	140 g	98 g
Number of features	8	12	16
Price	£140	£180	£220

Example: Model A is ....*cheaper*............. ....*than*.............. model B. (price)

34 Model A is much .... than model C. (weight)

35 Model C has twice .... features as model A.

36 Model A is .... model B. (price)

37 Model A is .... expensive.

38 Model C is .... (weight)

39 Model B is not .... model C. (price)

40 Model A has .... features .... model B.

41 Model C is .... expensive.

C Complete this report with the articles *a*, *an* or *the*, or leave the gap blank.

Example: This is ....*the*............. best food in the world!

McDonalds, ...⁴² fast food giant, is testing ....⁴³ new policy: 'all business is local'. ....⁴⁴ company is decentralising ....⁴⁵ marketing and ....⁴⁶ decision-making.

'You can't manage 25,000 restaurants in a centralised way,' says Jack Greenberg, ...⁴⁷ Chief Executive.

Year-end results show foreign sales and profit up by 10%. In .... ⁴⁸ US, profit was up by 13%.

Functions

Which phrases are most appropriate in a telephone conversation? Mark *all* the acceptable ones in each set.

49
a) James Watt's office. Good afternoon.
b) James Watt's office. Can I help you?
c) James Watt's office. What do you want?
d) James Watt's office.

50
a) Could I speak to James Watt, please?
b) I must speak to James Watt.
c) Give me James Watt.
d) Can I speak with James Watt, please?

51
a) He's not here.
b) Who are you?
c) Sorry, you can't.
d) I'm afraid he's not in the office at the moment.

52
a) Oh, could I leave a message then please?
b) Give him a message, will you?
c) Would it be possible to give him a message?
d) Well, could you ask him to call me back?

53
a) Certainly.
b) Yes, that's no problem.
c) What's your message?
d) What's your name?
e) Yes. Who's calling please?

Reading

Read the case study and answer the questions on the next page.

Daewoo and the art of customer focus

When Daewoo entered the UK car market in spring 1995 it was hardly known at all; its cars were technically average and had an unfashionable country of origin (Korea). With around 40 carmakers, the market was crowded. Less than half of these had market shares of over 1%. Many companies had a 'Buy UK' or 'Buy European' policy for their fleet purchases, which account for about half of all car purchases.

Since the mid 1970s, no new entrant to the UK car market had achieved more than a 1% market share. Yet Daewoo did exactly that in less than a year. We believe it did so by achieving its aim of being the most customer-focused car company in the UK.

Daewoo's market research revealed that its best target market would be drivers primarily interested in a car's ability to get from A to B reliably and cheaply. Surveys had shown that most motorists were afraid to visit car showrooms and found salespeople too aggressive. They believed that they were treated even worse after the sale. Further, Daewoo's research found that in its target segment, 84% of motorists believed that the treatment they got from the salesperson was at least as important as how they felt about the car itself.

Daewoo developed a new approach to selling:

1 They did not use dealers to sell their cars. By saving the money normally paid to dealers, Daewoo was able to offer higher specifications at a lower price.

2 Daewoo designed its car showrooms to be like high street stores, with free access to product informatio and a free café; salespeople were on a fixed salary and no negotiating on price was allowed.

3 The price included extensive guarantees and three years' free servicing.

4 Daewoo offered free collection and delivery as well as a courtesy car during servicing.

Daewoo's competitors had been unwilling or unable to rethink the way that they did business in the face of clear dissatisfaction in the market. This created a market opportunity that Daewoo was able to exploit.

Adapted from Mastering Marketing *(Financial Times)*

54 Which of the following sentences best summarises the content of the article?

    a) Daewoo's share of the UK car market is declining.

    b) Daewoo needs to research the UK car market more thoroughly.

    c) Daewoo understands what their customers really want.

    d) Daewoo sells cars by traditional methods.

55 Mark each of the following statements as T (true), F (false) or C (can't tell).

    a) Daewoo was not present in the UK car market until 1995.

    b) Cars from the Far East are not popular in the UK.

    c) There was very strong competition in the UK car market when Daewoo entered.

    d) Company cars account for approximately 50% of the UK car market.

    e) Only ten car manufacturers have a market share of more than 1%.

    f) Within a year, Daewoo had achieved a market share of more than 1%

56 Which of the following statements best describes Daewoo's cars, according to the information in the article?

    a) inexpensive in relation to the specifications

    b) technically very exciting

    c) luxury class

    d) unreliable

57 How does Daewoo sell its cars? Mark *all* the statements that are true.

    a) Offering salespeople large bonuses if they sell more.

    b) Making showrooms more friendly.

    c) Offering good after-sales service.

    d) Offering big discounts on price.

Writing

Below are some details of a trip you are planning to make to meet a colleague, Jack Lott, in London. Write an informal e-mail message to Jack explaining your travel arrangements. Jack has offered to meet you at the airport, so make sure he knows your flight arrival details.

ITINERARY

Outbound flight

Date: 6 April

Flight no: Crossair 9462

Geneva to London City Airport (NB: Not Heathrow)

Dep: 0850   Arr: 0910

Return flight

Date: 8 April

Flight no: Air France 341

London City Airport to Paris

Dep: 1635   Arr: 1825

Progress Test 2 (Units 5–8)

A You are going to hear part of a presentation about risks in international trade.

You have 30 seconds to read the questions below before you listen. You will hear the presentation twice.

1 The speaker is talking to:
   a) students of business administration.
   b) export managers from large companies.
   c) people who own their own businesses.
   d) business people without a lot of experience of exporting.

2 Mark *all* the topics the speaker mentions.
   a) receiving payment
   b) banking procedures
   c) avoiding disputes
   d) insurance
   e) exchange rate risk
   f) delivery problems

B You will now hear the next part of the presentation on risks in international trade.

You have 30 seconds to read the questions below before you listen. You will hear the presentation twice.

3 Of the four payment methods covered in the talk, which one does the speaker say has absolutely no risks for exporters?
   a) advance payment
   b) bills for collection
   c) letter of credit
   d) open trade account

4 Which of these payment methods does the speaker say has fewer risks for exporters?
   a) bills for collection
   b) letter of credit
   c) open trade account

5 Mark the following statements T (true) or F (false).
   a) Advance payment is risk-free for the importer.
   b) If advance payment is agreed, the exporter does not dispatch the goods until payment has been received.
   c) Documentary credit is another way to refer to a letter of credit.
   d) When the letter of credit payment method is used, the exporter sends all the documents direct to the importer.
   e) A letter of credit means that the importer's bank guarantees payment.
   f) The letter of credit method may involve some risks for the exporter if the documents are not correct.

Vocabulary

A Write a word which means the opposite of the word in italics in each of these sentences.

Example: It is a very *difficult* question.

............*easy*................

6 The company was very *hierarchical* in its organisation.

....

7 The risks involved in exporting to that country are very *high*.

....

8 The salesperson gave a very *interesting* presentation.

....

9 The buyers *refused* the consignment of jackets that arrived yesterday.

....

10 The service offered by their company was very *personal*.

....

B Complete the sentences by writing an appropriate word in each gap.

Example: The company ....*exports*............. goods to a lot of foreign countries.

11 The personnel department has received over forty .... for the post of assistant supervisor.

12 The job offers a lot of ....: you can choose your working hours and can take holidays when you want.

13 She's very ....: she wants to become a senior manager by the time she's forty.

14 After he was late for the meeting for the third time, his manager warned him to be more .... in future.

15 As he had no personal ...., he had to borrow capital from the bank to set up his business.

C Make word partnerships with the verbs on the left and the nouns on the right.

Example: write ⁀ a letter

16 break into   **a)** the delivery date
17 comply with   **b)** the market
18 meet   **c)** an order
19 place   **d)** a price
20 quote   **e)** regulations

D **Choose the best word to complete each of these sentences.**

21 In the 1980s, Mexico ended its policy of .... and opened up its economy to foreign investors.

    a) open borders   **b)** deregulation   **c)** dumping   **d)** protectionism

22 When exporting goods, it is essential to arrange .... in case the goods are lost or damaged in transit.

    a) a letter of credit   **b)** insurance cover   **c)** shipping documents

    d) a customs declaration

23 If a company has invested a lot of money in developing a product, it will take out a(n) .... to protect its right to profit from the sales of that product.

    a) patent   **b)** blueprint   **c)** prototype   **d)** order

24 Transport companies have to comply with strict .... when carrying dangerous materials.

    a) quotas   **b)** restrictions   **c)** regulations   **d)** barriers

25 One way that some countries protect their domestic industries is by imposing .... on all imports.

    a) tariffs   **b)** customs   **c)** payments   **d)** subsidies

26 The company decided not to proceed with Professor Grimshaw's idea because it was too ....

    a) feasible   **b)** viable   **c)** marketable   **d)** impractical

27 The employee who was sacked last week felt that his dismissal was unfair. He has decided to .... the company.

    a) test   **b)** court   **c)** sue   **d)** blame

28 When you apply for a job, you need a .... from your previous employer, or perhaps from your college professor.

    a) reference   **b)** recommendation   **c)** record   **d)** note

29 If you have a bank account, the bank sends you a monthly .... to inform you what has been debited from and credited to your account.

    a) sum   **b)** balance   **c)** bill   **d)** statement

30 A person who owns and runs a business, and is the only person responsible for it, is called a ....

    a) limited company   **b)** sole trader   **c)** entrepreneur   **d)** capitalist

Grammar

A **Complete the sentences with the correct form of the verb in brackets.**

Example: He ....*answered*............ (answer) the telephone and gave his name.

31 The terrorists are threatening to kill the hostages unless we

    .... (pay) them $1 million.

32 If we pay the terrorists, there .... (be) many more kidnappings in the future.

33 But if the hostages were killed, that .... (be) very bad for diplomatic relations.

34 Even if we .... (pay) the terrorists, we wouldn't be able to guarantee the safety of the hostages.

B Complete these sentences with the words in the box (one answer will be used twice).

if not	provided that	unless

Example: ....*Unless*.............. you pay within ten days, we will cancel all further deliveries.

35 .... you can give us a 10% discount, we will consider increasing our order.

36 Can you deliver by the end of the week? .... , we will have to cancel the order.

37 We cannot agree to the contract .... you offer us a full year's warranty.

38 We agree to pay $10 per unit .... you guarantee not to increase the price for at least a year.

C Complete these sentences by choosing an appropriate verb from the box and writing it in the correct form, active or passive.

advertise	draw up	fill out	invite	offer

Example: The form must ....*be filled out*........ in capitals.

39 When a company wishes to recruit a new employee, the post .... in the press.

40 People interested in applying for the post .... an application form.

41 The applications are screened and a short list of candidates ....

42 The selected candidates .... to an interview.

43 The chosen candidate .... the job.

D Rewrite the following phrases using an appropriate noun combination.

Example: a journey lasting two hours ..*a two-hour journey*.....................

44 a deal that is worth three million dollars

....

45 a document consisting of 200 pages

....

Functions **A** The conversation below takes place at an international sales conference. Complete the conversation with appropriate phrases from the list.

Pilar: Frank! ....46!

Frank: Hello, Pilar. ....47?

Pilar: ....48, thanks.

Frank: Pilar, ...49 Rudi Stein from the European Headquarters?

Pilar: Hello! ....50!

Rudi: ....51!

Frank: ....52 in the new Scalex project.

Pilar: That's right. We'll be working together on that.

Rudi: Perhaps we could meet and talk about it later. Right now

........................53.

Pilar: OK. ....54 this afternoon?

Rudi: Yes, ...55.

a) Nice to meet you
b) Nice to meet you too
c) How nice to see you again
d) How are you
e) I'm fine
f) That would be good
g) I'm afraid I have to go to a meeting
h) Maybe we could meet
i) I think you both have an interest
j) Can I introduce

B The expressions below are all commonly used in meetings. Match the expressions (56–65) with their functions (a–j).

56 I think we should move on now.
57 To sum up then …
58 That's it then, we've covered everything.
59 That sounds reasonable.
60 Let's get down to business.
61 I'm sorry I can't accept that.
62 How do you feel about that?
63 Could you let John finish, please?
64 If you order 5,000 or more, we can give you a discount.
65 When you say there are problems, what do you mean?

a) starting the meeting
b) dealing with interruptions
c) speeding up the meeting
d) asking for reactions
e) summarising
f) understanding clearly
g) making an offer
h) refusing an offer or suggestion
i) accepting an offer or suggestion
j) closing the meeting

Reading Read this case study about two international retailing companies.

Managing international retailing

1 Among international retailers, two have set the pace: Ikea, the Swedish furniture chain, and Toys "R" Us, the US toy retailer. They have built up worldwide 5 networks – Ikea in 28 countries, Toys "R" Us in 26 – of giant stores which have killed competition from local rivals.

Ikea is opening 12 new stores a year in cities including Frankfurt, Shanghai, 10 Chicago, and Wroclaw in Poland. A committee of senior executives at the group's international headquarters in Denmark oversees investment in new markets and the redesigning or 15 expansion of existing stores.

Responsibility for product development and purchasing lies with Ikea of Sweden, the original company that pioneered the 'blond' style of 20 Scandinavian furniture and furnishings which has gained a huge international following.

A third layer of country managers tailors the presentation and marketing 25 of those products in their home territories. Country managers usually assume control for day-to-day activities only when there are more than two stores in their region. They are allowed 30 some flexibility in choosing additional products which they think will meet local tastes.

At Toys "R" Us, by comparison, the fickle nature of children's choices 35 requires more latitude for local managers. Toy tastes vary significantly between different cultures, says Greg Staley, President of the company's international division. For example, 40 Asian families like educational toys, while American children are heavily influenced by Saturday morning television programmes. Some toys, such as Barbie dolls and Lego building sets, 45 do well everywhere. But others are less predictable.

Headquarters decides whether to open a new store but local managers take all the day-to-day decisions on what toys to 50 buy and in what quantities; how to market them, and how much to spend on advertising. 'We really do give them great latitude in the management of their business,' says Mr Staley.

Adapted from the Financial Times

Ⓐ Mark the sentences T (true) or F (false), according to the information in the case study.

66 Both Ikea and Toys "R" Us are strongly competitive in local markets around the world.

67 Ikea and Toys "R" Us have the same management structure for their international network.

68 Ikea's international headquarters are in Sweden.

69 Children in different countries like different kinds of toys.

70 Toys "R" Us local managers have more decision-making powers than Ikea local managers.

71 Ikea's country managers have more control when they are in charge of more than two stores in the same region.

B **Find the best explanation for each of these words and phrases as used in the case study.**

72 *have set the pace* (line 2)
    a) have been slow to expand
    b) have taken a lot of risks
    c) have provided a good example for others
    d) have been in competition with each other

73 *tailors* (line 24)
    a) takes full responsibility for
    b) creates ideas for
    c) carries out
    d) adapts or modifies

74 *fickle* (line 34)
    a) unpredictable
    b) expensive
    c) limited
    d) unchanging

75 *latitude* (line 35)
    a) restrictions
    b) assistance
    c) freedom
    d) guidance

Writing

You are a buyer of children's clothes and you work for a large department store in your country. You have just returned from a visit to a clothing manufacturer in Portugal. The Sales Manager of the Portuguese company, Mr Pereira, spent a whole day showing you around the factory and took you to lunch in a restaurant. You were impressed by the factory which has a high standard of quality and a very good range of items. You are planning to place an order with this company but you are waiting for your store to finalise the purchasing plan for the next quarter.

Write a letter to Mr Pereira and cover the following points.
- Thank him for showing you round and for the lunch.
- Express interest in the clothing he showed you.
- Tell him you are planning to order some items, but you are waiting for your company to finalise their purchasing plan.
- Tell him you will be in contact soon.

Progress Test 3 (Units 9–12)

You are going to hear part of a presentation given at a business management conference. The speaker describes a management case.
You will hear the presentation twice.

A Write a short answer (one word, a number or a phrase) to each of the questions below.

1 What was the business activity of the company in the case?

....

2 How many shops belonged to the company?

....

3 What was the title of the head of the company?

....

4 The shopkeepers were also shareholders in the company. True or false?

....

B Choose the best answer to each of the following questions.

5 What word was used to describe the way that meetings were run in the past?
   a) authoritarian
   b) efficient
   c) relaxed
   d) lengthy

6 A new head was brought in because …
   a) the company was old-fashioned.
   b) the former head had retired.
   c) profits were low.
   d) the company was nearly bankrupt.

7 The new head …
   a) had worked in this field of business all his life.
   b) already worked for this company.
   c) had not been a senior manager for long.
   d) was well known for making tough decisions.

8 The shopkeepers were not happy with the new head because …
   a) he didn't consult them about new decisions.
   b) he wasn't strong enough.
   c) his policies were not good for the company.
   d) he wasn't very friendly.

9 At the extraordinary meeting ...
   a) the atmosphere was very relaxed.
   b) people were very quiet.
   c) shareholders were unable to reach a decision.
   d) the board of management was replaced.

10 After the extraordinary meeting ...
   a) very little changed.
   b) the new management put new policies into practice.
   c) they returned to their old practices.
   d) people continued to be very unhappy.

Vocabulary

A **Make word partnerships with the verbs on the left and the nouns on the right.**

Example: write ——— a letter

11	achieve	a)	an agreement
12	carry out	b)	bribes
13	fill	c)	change
14	gain	d)	the customer base
15	hand out	e)	a debt
16	put out	f)	goals
17	reach	g)	market share
18	resist	h)	a post
19	widen	i)	a press release
20	write off	j)	a survey

B **For each of the words and phrases in italics, find another word with the same meaning which could also be used in the same sentence.**

Example: He didn't understand, so he asked the speaker to *clarify*.
   .explain........................

21 He wanted to be sure of getting the contract, so he offered the directors a *sweetener*.

   ....

22 The regulations regarding meat imports are very *severe*.

   ....

23 The decision to acquire a company at that stage was a very *courageous* one.

   ....

24 The company *is made up* of several divisions.

   ....

25 The dollar, the euro and the yen are all types of *money*.

   ....

C Choose the best word to complete each of these sentences.

26 Previously the company concentrated on just one business activity, but now they are planning to .... into new areas.
 a) vary   **b)** differ   **c)** diversify   **d)** differentiate

27 The company was not competitive with its huge workforce and it is now having to ....
 a) reduce   **b)** downturn   **c)** downsize   **d)** decline

28 .... are the total worth of a company, including everything it owns.
 a) Acquisitions   **b)** Assets   **c)** Goods   **d)** Valuables

29 We want to start selling in the Middle East, which is a completely new market for us, so we need a good local ....
 a) handler   **b)** transporter   **c)** district   **d)** distributor

30 Unfortunately the factory will have to close and all the workers will be made ....
 a) redundant   **b)** excessive   **c)** surplus   **d)** unemployable

31 Our two companies are going to work together in a(n) .... to produce the new model.
 a) merger   **b)** alliance   **c)** union   **d)** joint venture

32 He tried to cheat the bank by producing false documents, but now he has been found guilty of ....
 a) fraud   **b)** corruption   **c)** bribery   **d)** falsehood

33 Staff .... was very low following the changes made within the company.
 a) moral   **b)** morale   **c)** morality   **d)** mores

34 He lost a lot of money by .... on the stock exchange.
 a) running   **b)** crashing   **c)** bursting   **d)** speculating

35 The boom in share trading was following by heavy selling as the markets started to ....
 a) gain   **b)** rocket   **c)** collapse   **d)** recover

D Complete these sentences with appropriate words to describe the graph.
Write one word in each gap.

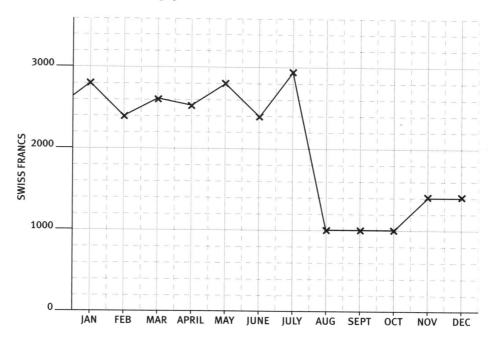

Example: In January, the price ....*stood*.............

....................*at*.................... 2,800 Swiss francs.

36 Sales in January ....

.... 10%.

37 The price .... in February to 2,400 Swiss francs.

38 From March to June, the price .... between 2,400 and
2,800 Swiss francs.

39 It ....

.... in July of 2,950 Swiss francs.

40 In August, there was a .... to
1000 Swiss francs.

41 The price reached a .... of
1,000 Swiss francs.

42 In September and October, the price remained .... at
1,000 Swiss francs.

43 In November, the price .... to
1,400 Swiss francs.

44 In December, the price ....

45 Over the year, the price has decreased .... about
50%.

Grammar

A **A salesman from Israel receives a telephone call from one of his customers. Write the correct form of the verbs in brackets in order to complete the story.**

Example: He ....*answered*............ (answer) the telephone and gave his name.

> Moshe Goldberg .... [46] (just leave) his office when he received a telephone call from Hans Lehman. 'I'm very worried,' Hans said. 'We .... [47] (not, receive) that delivery of machine tools that we ordered from you last week. You know you .... [48] (promise) that they would arrive today. But it's already 5 pm. What .... [49] (happen)?'
>
> Moshe said he .... [50] (not, know), but he would find out. He promised to call back as soon as he had some news. He phoned the transport agents right away. An embarrassed clerk at the agents' office explained what .... [51] (happen).
>
> The truck that .... [52] (carry) the consignment of machine tools to Germany .... [53] (have) an accident. Now the driver .... [54] (wait) on the side of the road for the emergency services to arrive. 'It .... [55] (take) several hours to put the truck back on the road again,' the clerk warned. Moshe Goldberg sighed and prepared to call Hans.

B **Match the beginning of each sentence (56–60) with the correct ending (a–e).**

56 Thank you	**a)** for not replying to your letter before.
57 I apologise	**b)** on helping you to prepare the report.
58 I insist	**c)** to seeing you soon.
59 They succeeded	**d)** in getting everything ready on time.
60 We look forward	**e)** for sending the documents.

C **Complete these sentences with the correct preposition.**

Example: I'm not interested ....*in*................. your product.

61 The sales manager wanted to increase the launch budget, but the finance manager didn't agree .... him.

62 I wrote asking for a quotation, but they haven't responded .... my request.

63 My customer in Dubai offered me a gold watch, but my company doesn't approve .... accepting gifts.

64 When you said 'those products', which products were you referring ....?

65 I believe we should sell off the unprofitable parts of the company and focus more .... our core business.

Functions

A **The expressions below are all commonly used in meetings. Match the expressions (66–75) with their functions (a–j).**

66 We've got to find out what our competitors are doing.

a) asking for facts

67 Alternatively, we could try speeding up production.

b) making a suggestion

68 The solution then is to discontinue the product.

c) balancing arguments

69 We should cut costs as far as possible.

d) expressing doubt

70 If we do that, everyone will have to work overtime.

e) identifying needs

71 Max, could you bring us up to date, please?

f) changing your approach

72 I'm worried about the motivation of the staff.

g) considering other options

73 Let's look at the pros and cons.

74 So the next thing is to find a new product.

h) discussing possible effects

i) making a decision

75 Let's look at this another way.

j) stating future action

B **Match these questions and suggestions (76–80) commonly used in meetings with the most appropriate response (a–e).**

76 What do you think?

a) Well, what I meant was …

77 Would you prepare a report on that?

b) I really can't agree – that's too late.

78 Could you explain your idea more clearly?

c) Yes, sure!

79 I think you should wait till next month.

d) That's right. We can't make a decision until we know the facts.

80 We really need more information on this.

e) I think it's an interesting idea – but it will be difficult to make it work.

Reading

Read the article on the next page about South African Breweries, a company which makes beer, then answer these questions.

81 Mark each of the following statements T (true) or F (false).

a) SAB has expanded rapidly outside South Africa since the end of apartheid.

b) SAB wants to leave the South African market.

c) SAB dominates the market in South Africa.

d) SAB has good opportunities for growth in its home market.

e) SAB sells beer in eastern Europe.

f) In South Africa, SAB is only involved in making beer.

g) SAB has been unable to make a profit from its activities in China.

h) There are many small brewers in the international market.

82 Why does SAB want to move to London? Mark *all* the answers that are correct.

a) The UK is its largest market.

b) It needs to be inside the European Union.

c) It wants to become part of the global beer industry.

d) It wants to compete equally with international brewers.

e) It hasn't been very successful in South Africa.

f) Exchange controls restrict the company in moving its funds abroad.

83 What is the meaning of *languish* (second to last line)? Choose the best answer.

a) expand further

b) lose strength

c) carry on in the same way

d) have to stop making beer

SAB moves to London

South African Breweries, the world's fourth largest brewer, is about to relocate to London where it hopes to raise capital by selling shares on the London Stock Exchange.

Since the fall of apartheid, the brewer has expanded rapidly outside South Africa into emerging markets in eastern Europe, Asia and the rest of sub-Saharan Africa. SAB's biggest move came in 1994 when the group jumped continents by entering the post-communist world of eastern Europe with the acquisition of a brewer in Hungary. It has since added brewing interests in Romania, Slovakia, Russia and Poland. It has also expanded into Asia with shares in four Chinese breweries through joint venture, and is negotiating to buy a fifth. 'Unlike most other brewers, we make money in China,' says Graham Mackay, Managing Director of SAB.

However, its ability to grow internationally is limited by exchange controls that restrict the use of cash from its South African brewing activities to fund overseas expansion. 'We must acquire access to the global share market to further growth in our international brewing business,' says Mr Mackay.

SAB is not about to pull out of South Africa, where it also owns the country's largest soft drinks bottling business and its largest hotels and gaming business. And it believes the core brewing business has room for further growth – despite its market share of 98%. 'More than 45% of the population is under 19 and yet to enter their beer-drinking years,' says Mr Mackay. 'More and more people are moving from the countryside into the towns. They earn more money and they choose to buy beer with it.'

One of the main purposes of listing the company on the London Stock Exchange is to fund further acquisitions in emerging markets, particularly in Poland. But the group also wants the freedom to be an active participant in the consolidation of the global brewing industry where the ten largest brewers control little more than a third of the market. 'We must participate in that process on equal terms with other international brewers or we will languish,' says Mr Mackay.

Adapted from the Financial Times

Writing

Read this short extract from a production department meeting and write a report about it. Note that not all the sentences have to be reported in full: some parts can be summarised.

Chair:	OK then. Item 3 on the Agenda is the cutting machine. John, could you tell us the background to this?
John:	Yes, well, as most people know, the cutting machine keeps breaking down. We've tried to get it repaired, but it's an old machine. Basically what we need is a new machine.
Everyone:	Yes! Definitely!
Chair:	OK. But should we get another machine of the same type? Perhaps this type is unreliable. Would it be a good idea to see what other machines are available?
Alice:	Yes – actually I've done a little research, and there are several possibilities. There are some new models on the market now. Perhaps we could consider one of those?
Chair:	Do you have any details about them? How much do they cost? Are they reliable?
Alice:	I have asked the manufacturers for some information but I haven't received any replies yet.
Chair:	Well, when you get the information, can you prepare a short report on it?
Alice:	Yes, I can do that.
Chair:	Good, then we can take a decision at our next meeting.
Alice:	All right.
Chair:	So – the next item on the Agenda ....

Exit Test (Units 13–16 and general review)

A You are going to hear a voicemail message giving information about some changes to the arrangements described in the letter below. There are three changes: write them in the space provided. Write the time and the activity.

You have one minute to read the letter before you hear the message. You will hear the message twice.

Dear Ms Greenall

Your visit to Socorro on 25 October

As promised, here is the programme for your visit to our company next week.

09:00	Pick up from your hotel
09:15	Coffee and presentation on the company by John Bissett and myself
10:00	Visit the plant
11:00	Meeting with Jack Phipps, Head of Product Development
12:30	Lunch
14:00	Meeting with Jenny Fowler, Head of Sales
16:00 approx.	Return to your hotel

We hope this programme suits you and look forward to welcoming you at Socorro on Wednesday next week.

Yours sincerely

Trudy Ferrier

Trudy Ferrier
Customer Relations Officer

---

1 ....

2 ....

3 ....

B You are going to hear a conversation between two colleagues, Peter and Jenny.

Before you listen, you have 30 seconds to read through the questions below. You will hear this conversation *once only*, so you may like to make notes while you listen. You will have time to complete your answers after listening.

4 Which department do Peter and Jenny work in?
   a) sales
   b) finance
   c) production
   d) R & D

5 How many items have Hadley's ordered?
   ....

6 Which models have been ordered?
   a) the most expensive
   b) several different ones
   c) the latest ones
   d) the cheapest

7 What is the value of the order?
   ....

8 When is Peter hoping that Hadley's will place another similar order?
   ....

9 Which of the following statements are true? Mark *all* those that are correct.
   a) Jenny is worried that they won't be able to produce the goods on time.
   b) Peter hasn't talked to the production department yet.
   c) Peter is sure they can deliver on time.
   d) Jenny is pleased because the sales results will be good this year.
   e) Jenny is disappointed that the order wasn't bigger.

10 What is the relationship with the buyers, Hadley's?
   a) They have been customers for a long time.
   b) They are new customers.
   c) This order is a one-off.
   d) They place regular orders every six months.

Vocabulary

A Select the best word or phrase from the next page to complete this letter to the Public Relations Officer at Air Manuko.

Dear Mr Morgan

We ....[11] a report expressing our dissatisfaction with Air Manuko over the cancellation of our tickets on a recent visit to Manuko. This error ....[12] some considerable worry and trouble during our visit, as well as incurring extra costs.

As we were ....[13] to travel by air from Katawe to Harristown (in spite of having ....[14] and paid for this flight three months before), we were ....[15] to go by road, the cost of which was $120.

We would now like to ask whether this cost could be ....[16]. We attach copies of our flight vouchers and the ....[17] for the road transfer.

We ....[18] to hearing from you about this matter.

Yours sincerely

Christopher Bartlett

---

11 **a)** enclose   **b)** submit   **c)** include   **d)** send

12 **a)** raised   **b)** caused   **c)** gave   **d)** made

13 **a)** prevented   **b)** disabled   **c)** unable   **d)** incapable

14 **a)** cancelled   **b)** recorded   **c)** registered   **d)** booked

15 **a)** obliged   **b)** made   **c)** having   **d)** caused

16 **a)** paid back   **b)** reduced   **c)** reimbursed   **d)** returned

17 **a)** fare   **b)** quote   **c)** recipe   **d)** receipt

18 **a)** expect   **b)** hope   **c)** are waiting   **d)** look forward

B Select the best word or phrase to complete this notice in a company newsletter.

> Our Managing Director, Daniel Hawkes, has been offered a position as Vice President of our parent company, and is ....[19] after more than 11 years with TDI. During his time as Managing Director, he has shown outstanding leadership ....[20]. He has sometimes had to make some ....[21] decisions, but he is known to be caring and concerned for his staff.
>
> Mr Hawkes built up the company from a small business with a fragile bank balance to a ....[22] concern. Last year, we achieved a ....[23] turnover, thanks to his energy and ....[24].
>
> Mr Hawkes will be greatly missed by all, and we wish him every success in his new role. It is not yet known who will ....[25] his position in TDI.

19 **a)** retiring   **b)** being dismissed   **c)** resigning   **d)** parting

20 **a)** qualities   **b)** character   **c)** aspects   **d)** attractions

21 **a)** tough   **b)** strong   **c)** heavy   **d)** serious

22 **a)** fading   **b)** dwindling   **c)** thriving   **d)** flowering

23 **a)** maximum   **b)** record   **c)** top   **d)** leading

24 **a)** challenge   **b)** power   **c)** force   **d)** drive

25 **a)** fill out   **b)** fill up   **c)** fulfil   **d)** fill

Grammar

A **A sales manager sent this memo to his sales team. The mistakes have been underlined. Write the corrections in the spaces provided.**

Example: The company <u>is producing</u> 4,000 units per year.
...*produces*......

> As you know, we have been asked to go and present our proposals for the Russian contract, and the buyers have scheduled the presentation <u>to</u>[26] next Wednesday afternoon. We have a lot to prepare before then.
>
> <u>Already we have sent</u>[27] a written proposal, so we <u>wouldn't</u>[28] have to repeat the same information. What we must do is emphasise our key strengths and show how we are different from and better than our competitors.
>
> <u>We hold</u>[29] a meeting to plan the presentation tomorrow at 10 a.m. and I would like <u>that you come</u>[30] with some good ideas. There is strong competition for this contract and if we <u>won't</u>[31] make the right impression next Wednesday, we could lose it. Be there <u>on</u>[32] 10 o'clock sharp, please.

26 ....

27 ....

28 ....

29 ....

30 ....

31 ....

32 ....

B **Choose the best answer to complete each gap in this article.**

> America Online, the leading internet service provider, said yesterday that its
>
> customers ....[33] $1.2bn in purchases between November 26 and
>
> December 27. ....[34] estimates vary widely, the figures were
>
> generally higher ....[35] expected as more and more buyers used the
>
> internet to purchase toys, books, clothing and travel services. AOL's figures
>
> ....[36] important to the online industry ....[37] there are
>
> more than 15m AOL members and they account for nearly half of all online
>
> transactions. AOL also ....[38] that 17 December was its
>
> ....[39] shopping day to date, with about $36m in sales. Shares in
>
> AOL ....[40] to $151 on the New York Stock Exchange yesterday.

33	**a)** were spending	**b)** had been spending	**c)** had spent	**d)** have spent
34	**a)** Despite	**b)** Although	**c)** However	**d)** Whereas
35	**a)** as	**b)** than	**c)** like	**d)** that
36	**a)** are	**b)** were	**c)** have been	**d)** had been
37	**a)** due to	**b)** because of	**c)** because	**d)** owing to
38	**a)** reported	**b)** have reported	**c)** had reported	**d)** are reporting
39	**a)** busy	**b)** most busy	**c)** busiest	**d)** busier
40	**a)** felt	**b)** fell	**c)** have fell	**d)** had fallen

Functions

A Match the responses on the right to the sentences on the left.

41 I just got that new job.

42 Thank you so much.

43 I'm afraid I've spilt coffee on your desk!

44 Can I help you to carry those books?

45 May I use your phone?

a) Don't worry about it.

b) That's kind of you.

c) Please do.

d) Not at all.

e) Congratulations!

B In the following groups of sentences, the speaker is either complaining or responding to a complaint.

46 Which is the most *forceful* of these complaints?

   a) I'm sorry but I'm not satisfied with this product.

   b) There is a small problem with this product.

   c) Unfortunately, we had some problems with this product.

   d) The product doesn't seem to work very well.

47 Which is the most *polite* of these responses?

   a) What's the problem then?

   b) I'm very sorry to hear about your problem.

   c) You could be using it incorrectly.

   d) It's not our fault if the equipment wasn't installed correctly.

C Put these parts of a negotiation in the correct order. Write the letter for each sentence on the appropriate line.

The dialogue begins with the buyer saying: 'OK. We have an agreement on price. Let's talk about delivery ...'

48 **Supplier:** ....

49 **Buyer:** ....

50 **Supplier:** ....

51 **Buyer:** ....

52 **Supplier:** ....

53 **Buyer:** ....

54 **Supplier:** ....

55 **Buyer:** ....

56 **Supplier:** ....

57 **Buyer:** ....

58 **Supplier:** ....

a) I'm afraid the earliest we could deliver would be in six weeks' time.

b) Well, we might be able to do something there – but I'd have to check with our Production Manager.

c) We can't possibly wait that long. Isn't there some way we can speed things up?

d) Could you arrange delivery by the end of the month?

e) When could you let me know?

f) OK, but if we can't find a solution, we may have to look for another supplier.

g) I'll give you a call tomorrow.

h) That's a possibility, but we really need to save more than four days. What about your production schedule: could you give our order priority?

i) We could transport the goods by air. That would save about four days. But it would also cost more.

j) I understand that, Mr Rupp. We'll see what we can do.

k) Go ahead.

Reading

A Read these four short newspaper articles.

1

South Korea's carmakers yesterday revealed plunging sales figures for last year amid the worst economic recession for decades. Hyundai Motor, the biggest carmaker, reported sales down 29.4%. Exports fell year on year by 4.9%, while domestic sales plummeted 52.3%.

Daewoo Motor fared a little better, seeing an overall drop in sales of 7.8%. Exports rose 20.4% on the strength of robust sales of its Matiz mini-car. Domestic sales slumped 44.4%. Financially-troubled Kia Motors, soon to be taken over by Hyundai, saw a 33% drop in sales led by a 53.3% fall among domestic buyers. Exports fell 10.9%.

Adapted from the Financial Times

2

Expectations that US car sales will remain strong this year have prompted Germany's leading carmakers, which dominate luxury imports, to forecast new sales records for the coming year.

Jens Neumann, Volkswagen board member for North America, said sales should reach almost 300,000 units. Last year, VW sold 218,000 cars, its highest figure since 1981, when it still built vehicles in the US. 'We believe we can continue to grow at double-digit rates,' he predicted.

The strong US performance underpinned an 11% rise in VW's world sales to more than 4.7m units, taking VW's world market share from 10.4 to 11.4%.

Adapted from the Financial Times

3

Société Générale de Surveillance, the Switzerland-based group that is the world's biggest testing and inspection company, is facing one of the toughest tests in its 120-year history. Profits have collapsed, the dividend has been axed and the group can no longer rely on its lucrative government contract business, which provided three-quarters of last year's profits, to subsidise under-performing operations.

The group has a new Chairman, a new Chief Executive, and an almost completely new board of directors, after Elisabeth Salina Amorini, a member of one of the company's founding families, was forced to step down as Chairman in September.

SGS also has a new corporate strategy, which involves cutting up to 3,500 jobs, or 12% of its staff.

Adapted from the Financial Times

4

Full-year profits at Xaar, the Cambridge-based ink jet printing technology group, will be 'significantly below market expectations'.

In September, the directors said that year-end results would be dependent on the outcome and timing of licence fee negotiations. In the event, no new licences were signed last year.

Last July, Xaar initiated legal proceedings against Calcomp, claiming that the US company's CrystalJet line of ink jet printers infringed Xaar's patents.

Xaar shares yesterday rose 4.5p to 60.5p.

Adapted from the Financial Times

59 Match each of these headlines with one of the articles, 1, 2, 3 or 4.

    a) Car sales tumble   ....

    b) New board faces hard decisions   ....

    c) End of year results expected to be down ....

    d) Record sales for the coming year   ....

60 Which article reports on each of these items? Choose 1, 2, 3 or 4.

    a) An increase in market share.   ....

    b) Plans to reduce the number of staff in
        a company.   ....

    c) An increase in the share price of a
        company despite its falling profit.   ....

    d) A comparison in the performance of
        companies in the same industry sector. ....

    e) A company engaged in a law suit.   ....

B Read the article *Ice cream wars in Vietnam*. **Some parts of the text have been taken out. These extracts are listed on the next page. Complete each gap with the appropriate extract. One of the sentences does not belong in any of the gaps.**

Ice cream wars in Vietnam

The buying patterns of the Vietnamese suggest they find it hard to resist the temptation of foreign consumer brands. ....⁶¹

When it comes to ice cream and other milk products, however, they are more often loyal to the state-owned dairy company, Vinamilk. Claiming over two-thirds of the country's market for milk products, ...⁶²

As foreign dairy companies begin to target the Vietnamese market, however, Vinamilk is facing an uphill struggle to maintain its market share. At stake is a relatively small but expanding market. ....⁶³ But this is still below the modest five litres per person which is consumed in China.

Ms Ha is one of a mainly female management team at Vinamilk battling to fight off the foreign competition. 'It's obvious that a newcomer will take some market share,' she says. 'Especially one with a foreign name, which Vietnamese customers will tend to prefer.'

Among the competitors are Unilever's Wall's brand and the Foremost Dairy Company of the Netherlands. Foremost, a subsidiary of Freisland, opened the competition when it began a few years ago operating a $30m joint-venture dairy near Ho Chi Minh City, producing condensed and powdered milk and drinking yoghurt. ....⁶⁴

Rien de Groot, General Director of Vietnam Foremost Dairy, says Foremost has already taken a third of the market for tinned condensed milk in less than two years. ....⁶⁵

Adapted from the Financial Times

---

a) Last year, Unilever began producing Wall's ice cream at a $22m plant, also in Ho Chi Minh City.

b) In addition, Foremost already claims roughly half the market for the two powdered milk products it produces in Vietnam.

c) Average annual consumption of milk products per head in Vietnam stands at about three litres, up from less than a litre in the early 1990s.

d) They would sooner drink a Coke or a Pepsi than the local Festi Cola and would smoke a Marlboro cigarette rather than the domestic Vinataba brand.

e) But the taste for foreign brands is not the only handicap facing the management team.

f) Vinamilk is regularly hailed in the official media as one of the state sector's few success stories.

Writing

Study this chart which compares the sales figures for three similar products in the same market sector. Also read the report of a customer survey.

Write a short paragraph of about 150 to 200 words to report on the sales of these products.

In your paragraph, you should:

- describe changes in the sales of products A, B and C over the last year.

- give reasons for the different success rates of the three products.

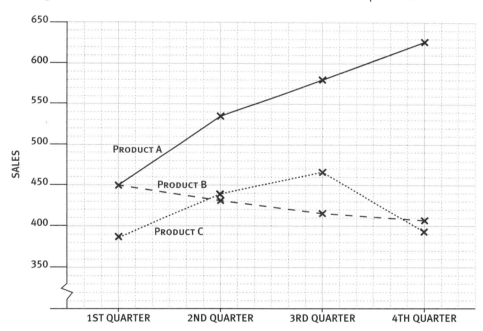

REPORT OF CUSTOMER SURVEY

- Many buyers reported that they prefer A because it's a new product and is more up to date than the others.

- Many buyers bought B before, but have now changed to A because it looks more attractive.

- Most buyers think that C is really the best product, but it's too expensive. Some bought it for a time when the price was reduced during a special offer.

Speaking

You are going to have a ten minute oral test. You should prepare both items before starting the test. You will have five minutes to prepare.

A Study the information and be ready to carry out a role-play. In the role-play, you should cover the following:

- Greet Mr/Mrs Harris and introduce yourself.
- Make small talk for one or two minutes. Be ready to answer questions about your travel to Britain, your length of stay in Britain, if you have been to Britain before and so on.
- Answer questions about your company using the information given.
- Ask similar questions about *HG Supplies*.

You are a representative of a Singaporean company called *Hi-Tek*, which produces medical equipment. You are on a marketing visit to Britain and you are going to visit a hospital supply company called *HG Supplies*, which is based in London. Your contact there is Mr/Mrs Harris. Below are some details about your company and job. You can use your own name.

Your company:	Hi-Tek
Your job title:	Export Manager
Headquarters:	Singapore
Products:	Equipment for medical testing for use in hospitals using advanced technology
Size of company:	Medium
Employees:	1,240, of which 150 are employed in research and development
Manufacturing plants:	In Singapore and in Taiwan, employing a total of 890 workers

---

B Study the list of important qualities for salespeople. You will be asked to give your opinion about these. Be ready to say which you think is the most important, which is next most important and which is least important. Give some reasons why you have this opinion.

Note: There are no right or wrong answers. The examiner will only be interested in how well you can express your opinions.

Important qualities for salespeople
- Smart appearance
- Good communication skills
- Excellent product knowledge
- A charismatic personality
- Energetic
- Highly motivated

Answer Key

Entry Test

Listening (10 marks)

See page 41 for audio script.

  1 b, d (4 marks max.: deduct 1 for each mistake)
  2 b, d (3 marks max.: deduct 1 for each mistake)
  3 a, c and e (3 marks max.: deduct 1 for each mistake)

Vocabulary (20 marks)

A **4** competitors
    5 agreement
    6 economic
    7 product
    8 organisation

B **9** h   **10** f   **11** a   **12** i   **13** d
    14 b **15** g **16** c **17** j **18** e

C **19** c   **20** e   **21** a   **22** b   **23** d

Grammar (25 marks)

A **24** Can *or* May
    25 from *or* with
    26 have
    27 will

B **28** Please to meet you (too) *or* Nice to meet you *or* How do you do
    29 Did you have
    30 Would you like
    31 Do you take *or* Would you like

C **32** b **33** c **34** b **35** b **36** d **37** a

D **38** b **39** d **40** a

E **41** c **42** b **43** d

F **44, 47** and **48** (5 marks max.: deduct 1 for each mistake)

Reading (15 marks)

  49 b **50** g **51** c **52** h **53** j
  54 e **55** i **56** d **57** a **58** f
  59 a and e (5 marks max.: deduct 1 for each mistake)

Total marks: 70

Progress Test 1

Listening (10 marks)

See page 41 for audio script.

  1 1st event: b
      2nd event: e
      3rd event: g
      4th event: f
      5th event: c
      6th event: d
      7th event: a
      (5 marks max.: deduct 1 for each mistake)
  2 a) 1980s
      b) 50 million
      c) 1.5 billion
      d) 50
      (1 mark for each correct answer)
  3 a and d (1 mark only if both correct)

Vocabulary (20 marks)

A **4** d   **5** c   **6** e   **7** f   **8** b   **9** a

B **10** complained
    11 survey
    12 loyal
    13 consortium
    14 media

C **15** b   **16** a   **17** b   **18** c

D **19** good quality
    20 low priced *or* reasonably priced *or* good value for money
    21 well made
    22 well known
    23 modern *or* up to date

Grammar (25 marks)

A **24** was
    25 have been
    26 has risen
    27 cost
    28 were
    29 conducted
    30 showed
    31 have increased
    32 have targeted
    33 has not increased

B **34** heavier
    35 as many
    36 less expensive than
    37 the least
    38 the lightest
    39 as expensive as
    40 fewer ... than
    41 the most

C **42** the
    43 a
    44 The
    45 –
    46 –
    47 the
    48 the

Functions (5 marks)

49 a, b and d
50 a and d
51 d
52 a, c and d
53 a, b and e
(1 mark per question only if *all* the answers are given correctly in each question)

Reading (10 marks)

54 c
55 a) T   b) C   c) T   d) T   e) C   f) T
(6 marks max.: deduct 1 for each mistake)
56 a
57 b and c (2 marks max.: deduct 1 for each mistake)

Writing (10 marks)

See page 43 for model answer.

Award marks for writing as follows:
Including all the facts clearly (printed in italics in the model answer)   4
Politeness
(thanking, looking forward to meeting)   3
Deduct half a mark for each *major* grammatical mistake (small inaccuracies can be tolerated as this is e-mail)   3

Total marks: 80

Progress Test 2

Listening (10 marks)

See page 41 for audio scripts.

A **1** d
    2 a, c and e (1 mark only if all are correct)

B **3** a
    4 b
    5 a) F   b) T   c) T   d) F   e) T   f) T
    (6 marks max.: deduct 1 for each mistake)

Vocabulary (25 marks)

A **6** flat
    7 low
    8 boring *or* dull
    9 accepted
   10 impersonal

B **11** applications
   12 flexibility
   13 ambitious
   14 punctual
   15 assets

C **16** b   **17** e   **18** a   **19** c   **20** d

D **21** d   **22** b   **23** a   **24** c   **25** a
   26 d   **27** c   **28** a   **29** d   **30** b

Grammar (15 marks)

A **31** pay
    32 will be or could be or may be
    33 would be
    34 paid

B **35** Provided that
    36 If not
    37 unless
    38 provided that

C **39** is advertised
    40 fill out
    41 is drawn up
    42 are invited
    43 is offered

D **44** a three-million dollar deal
    45 a 200-page document

Functions (20 marks)

A **46** c   **47** d   **48** e   **49** j   **50** a
    51 b   **52** i   **53** g   **54** h   **55** f

B **56** c   **57** e   **58** j   **59** i   **60** a
    61 h   **62** d   **63** b   **64** g   **65** f

Reading (10 marks)

A **66** T   **67** F   **68** F   **69** T   **70** T   **71** T

B **72** c   **73** d   **74** a   **75** c

Writing (10 marks)

See page 43 for model answer.

Award marks for writing as follows:
Including all the points clearly (printed in italics in the model answer)   2
Politeness (thanking, showing appreciation, closing)   4
Deduct half a mark for each *major* grammatical mistake   4

Total marks: 90

Progress Test 3

Listening (10 marks)

See page 42 for audio script.

A
1. selling flowers
2. about 2,500
3. president
4. True

B 5 c   6 c   7 d   8 a   9 d   10 a

Vocabulary (35 marks)

A 11 f   12 j   13 h   14 g   15 b
16 i   17 a   18 c   19 d   20 e

B
21. bribe
22. strict
23. brave
24. consists
25. currency

C 26 c   27 c   28 b   29 d   30 a
31 d   32 a   33 b   34 d   35 c

D
36. went up by
37. fell or dropped or decreased
38. fluctuated
39. reached a peak
40. dramatic or sharp/fall or drop or decrease
41. low point
42. steady or constant
43. went up
44. levelled off or remained stable or remained constant
45. by

Grammar (20 marks)

A
46. was just leaving
47. haven't received
48. promised
49. (has) happened
50. didn't know
51. had happened
52. was carrying
53. had had
54. was waiting
55. will take or may take

B 56 e   57 a   58 b   59 d   60 c

C
61. with
62. to
63. of
64. to
65. on

Functions (15 marks)

A 66 e   67 g   68 i   69 b   70 h
71 a   72 d   73 c   74 j   75 f
B 76 e   77 c   78 a   79 b   80 d

Reading (10 marks)

81. a) T   b) F   c) T   d) T   e) T
f) F   g) F   h) T
(8 marks max.: deduct 1 for each mistake)
82. c, d and f (1 mark only if *all* are correct)
83. b

Writing (10 marks)

See page 43 for model answer.

Award marks for writing as follows:
Including all the key points clearly
(printed in italics in the model answer)   4
Correct use of reported speech forms
(deduct half a mark for each mistake)   3
Deduct half a mark for each *major*
grammatical mistake   3

Total marks: 100

Exit Test

Listening (10 marks)

See page 42 for audio scripts.

A
1. 08:45   Pick up from your hotel
2. 09:00   Coffee and presentation
3. 14:00   Meeting with Peter Fisher

B
4. a
5. 15
6. a
7. 200,000 dollars
8. in six months
9. a, c and d (1 mark only if *all* are correct)
10. b

Vocabulary (15 marks)

A 11 a   12 b   13 c   14 d   15 a
16 c   17 d   18 d

B 19 c   20 a   21 a   22 c   23 b
24 d   25 d

Grammar (15 marks)

A
26. for
27. We have already sent
28. don't or won't
29. We are holding
30. you to come
31. don't
32. at

B 33 c   34 b   35 b   36 a   37 c
38 a   39 c   40 b

Functions (18 marks)

A 41 e   42 d   43 a   44 b   45 c
B 46 a   47 b
C 48 k   49 d   50 a   51 c   52 i   53 h
54 b   55 e   56 g   57 f   58 j

Reading *(12 marks)*

A 59 a) 1   b) 3   c) 4   d) 2
   (2 marks if all correct; 1 mark if two texts are incorrectly
   matched)
   60 a) 2   b) 3   c) 4   d) 1   e) 4
   (5 marks max.: deduct 1 for each mistake)
B 61 d   62 f   63 c   64 a   65 b
   (Sentence e is not used.)

Writing *(15 marks)*

See page 43 for model answer.

Award marks for writing as follows:
Including all the key points clearly
(printed in italics in the model answer)   4
Correct use of appropriate language to
describe trends and make comparisons
(deduct half a mark for each mistake)   8
Overall clarity, organisation of points and
readability   3

Speaking *(15 marks)*

See page 44 for guidelines for the examiner.

Note: It is recommended that the oral test be recorded on tape
for analysis afterwards. Oral performance should always be
assessed by at least *two* teachers. In the event of disagreement,
award a score midway between the two (if two assessors), or
take an average (if three or more assessors).

Award marks for speaking as follows:
Use of polite social language to greet,
introduce and make small talk   2
Ability to understand and react
appropriately to questions or remarks   2
Ability to give clear and accurate
information   2
Ability to ask clear and accurate questions
about *HG Supplies*   1
Ability to express clearly an opinion   1
Ability to support an opinion with clear
logical reasons   1
Overall fluency and confidence in speaking   2
Range of vocabulary and expression   1
Clarity of pronunciation   2
Ability to expand on an answer (not just
give a minimal response to a question)   1

The oral performance of candidates with a pass score of 8 or
more can be described as follows:

The candidate can use English to communicate effectively and
consistently, with few hesitations or uncertainties.

Description based on level 7 of the English Speaking Union's
Framework of Examination Levels.

Total marks: 100

Audio Scripts

Entry Test

Play the conversation twice.

A What do you think about moving to the new offices then? Personally, I'm not keen on the idea. I like being here in the centre of town and being able to go out to the shops in the lunch hour. And I'll really miss going to our favourite café for lunch. You know we'll have to eat in the office canteen because there'll be nowhere else to go.

B Well, yes. It won't be as nice being outside town. But think how much more practical the new building will be. We'll have more space, more light, more modern conveniences. You know how small that old building is now that the company's expanded. In fact you're always complaining about the size of your office!

A Yes, that's true, I suppose. But I will have a problem getting to work. I'll have to go by car because the bus service out there is terrible!

B Yes, I agree. And not everyone has a car. Maybe we should talk to the management about that. They should organise a company bus service for all the staff.

Progress Test 1

Play the speech twice.

Not many companies can say they have survived because they decided to go global but Cemex is certainly one of them.
Back in 1995, there was a financial crisis in Mexico. The value of the peso fell sharply and income from our domestic operations was cut by 50%. It could have been the end of us. It was our foreign subsidiaries that saved us. The income from our overseas plants brought in enough money to help us stay in business.
We decided to become a global company in the mid 1980s. At that time, Mexico had just opened up its economy to foreign investors. We suddenly found that we were competing with very large international companies. We had to become large and international as well or we would end up being purchased by a bigger company.
Our first step in globalising was to focus on our core business: cement. So we sold off all our other industrial projects and bought two domestic competitors in the cement business. Then we started to acquire companies overseas. First we bought two cement producers in the US; and later we also acquired plants in Spain, Venezuela and Colombia. We invested over one and a half billion dollars in modernising the plants we had acquired. As a result, our production went up from nine million tonnes to fifty million tonnes in just ten years. And in every plant we increased our profit margins.
Now Cemex is looking to expand still further. We recently acquired a cement plant in the Philippines and we are looking for more opportunities to buy in Asia. Now is definitely the right time to buy.

Progress Test 2

A Play section A of the presentation twice.

Section A

Good afternoon, ladies and gentlemen. I'm very pleased to be here with you today to talk about risks in international trade. I know that many of you have small and medium-sized businesses, and that you haven't exported before. As you enter international markets, you need to be aware that there are a number of things that can cause problems.
In particular, I'd like to focus on the following points during my talk: firstly, payment. How can you make sure that you will receive payment for your goods, on time and in full? Secondly, exchange rate risk. As you know, you can lose a lot of money if your customer is paying in US dollars and then the value of the dollar falls before you receive the payment. How can you protect yourself against losing money in this way? Thirdly, disputes. How can you avoid getting into costly and time-consuming disagreements with your buyers over such problems as delivery, quality and, of course, payment?
So those are the main points that I'll be covering today. Let's start with the first one. Payment.
Basically, there are four payment methods which can be used when exporting goods: advance payment, letter of credit, bills for collection and open trade account.

B Play section B of the presentation twice.

Section B

Let's deal first with advance payment. This is ideal for the exporter. You ask your customer to send the money before you dispatch the goods. That way you know that you'll get your money and there's absolutely no risk to you. However, there is a lot of risk for the customer because he doesn't know if or when you might send him the goods. So there are not many situations where the customer will agree to this method.
So what about the second method? Letter of credit, or documentary credit as it is also known. This is a reasonably safe method for the exporter. What happens is the buyers ask their bank to guarantee payment to the exporter. As soon as the exporting company has dispatched the goods, they must present all the documents to their bank to prove that the goods are on their way and that everything has been done according to the sales agreement. Then the exporter's bank passes the documents on to the importer's bank. This bank makes the payment by letter of credit – so the exporter can receive their money and the importer can receive the goods. This method is particularly low risk for the exporter, although you must make sure that you present the correct documents and that you comply with all the terms and conditions of the agreement. If there is any kind of mistake, you could lose the protection of the letter of credit. So this method has fewer risks than the open account or bills for collection, but is not as risk-free as advance payment, from your point of view.
Now let's move on to the third payment method ...

Progress Test 3

Play the presentation twice.

I'd now like to describe a case concerning a company whose business is selling flowers. Basically, the company consists of about 2,500 flower shops, all over the country, all of them leased to shopkeepers. There is a board of management with a president to oversee the business. The shopkeepers are all shareholders in the company and are entitled to go and vote at the annual shareholders' meetings.

Now, in the past, this company was run like a family business. Everyone was very friendly, meetings were very relaxed. There were lots of social gatherings where the shopkeepers could meet and get to know each other. And all the shops retained quite a lot of independence and made their own decisions about their day-to-day operations. But the company as a whole was not doing well. Profits across the country were down, and it was felt that some changes would have to be made. So, a new president was brought in from outside the company. He was not an expert at selling flowers, but he was a very experienced manager with a reputation for making tough decisions and getting companies out of trouble.

Well, once this new man took over the running of the company, a lot of things changed very rapidly. The shopkeepers were told that they all had to buy their flowers from the same supplier. All the shops had to look the same. Opening hours had to be the same. And certain minimum standards were set which everyone had to follow. The shopkeepers didn't like this at all. They felt that decisions were being taken by the board and they were no longer being consulted. They resented this new authoritarian style of management very much.

So some of the shopkeepers organised an extraordinary meeting and everyone was invited. A lot of people attended. At the meeting, the atmosphere was very hostile. Shareholders made speeches about what they saw as the defects of the management team and in particular they complained about the new president. People got angrier and angrier. Eventually, a vote was taken and it was decided unanimously that all the directors should be sacked. In their place, they elected a new board from amongst themselves. A coup had taken place.

The interesting thing is that the new board didn't actually change the policies very much. All the actions that had been taken by the unpopular president and his team were continued. They continued the practice of standardising the shops and buying from a common supplier, because these policies actually made a lot of sense. So you see, what people objected to was not the changes in themselves, but the way in which those changes were made. And this is a very good lesson for us all.

Exit Test

A Play the voicemail message twice.

Hello. This is Trudy Ferrier from Socorro. Er – I'm calling because we have had to make some changes to the programme for your visit on Wednesday. First – is it OK if we pick you up from your hotel at 8.45 instead of 9 o'clock? It's because our driver has to pick up someone else afterwards. So we'll start the presentation at 9 o'clock. I hope that's all right.

Also, unfortunately, Jenny Fowler won't be able to meet you in the afternoon as she's had to go to Hungary this week. So you'll meet the Assistant Head of Sales – that's Peter Fisher.

I just thought I'd let you know about these changes. OK. I look forward to seeing you on Wednesday. Bye.

B Play the conversation once only.

Peter   Hi Jenny! Great news – we just received an order from Hadley's!

Jenny   Hadley's! You've been chasing them for months! Well done! What have they ordered?

Peter   Fifteen top of the range models. The total order is worth over 200,000 dollars. They want them within one month.

Jenny   Oh! Can the production department handle it?

Peter   Oh yes – I've already talked to them. That's no problem. They're going to give priority to this order. I stressed that Hadley's could be very good customers in the long term. You know they hinted that there could be another similar order in six months' time. So we have to get everything right on this order – make sure we deliver on time and so on.

Jenny   Another order in six months! That will really boost our turnover this year. I think this calls for a celebration, don't you?

Model Answers to Writing Tasks

Entry Test

There is no writing task in the Entry Test.

Progress Test 1

Dear Jack

Here are the details of my travel to London on *6 April*. I will arrive at *London City Airport (not Heathrow)* at *09:10*. My flight number is *Crossair 9462*. I will depart on *8 April for Paris at 16:35*.

It is very kind of you to offer to meet me. I am very much looking forward to my visit.

Best regards

Progress Test 2

Dear Mr Pereira

I am writing to thank you for your kind hospitality during my visit to your company. *The visit around your factory* was very interesting and I was impressed by the high quality standards that you maintain. Many thanks also for the delicious *lunch*. It was good of you to give up so much of your *time*.

You have a *good range of children's fashion items* and I am certainly hoping to be able to *place an order* with you in the near future. However, I must *first wait for my company to finalise the purchasing plan* for the next quarter.

I will be in *contact with you again as soon as I can*.

Yours sincerely,

Progress Test 3

3   The cutting machine

John explained the background to this item. He said that *the cutting machine kept breaking down*. They had *tried to get it repaired* but it was an old machine. *Everyone agreed that a new machine was needed*.

The chair asked *whether we should get another machine of the same type*. He said that *perhaps this type was unreliable* and suggested *finding out what other machines were available*.

Alice said *she had done some research* and that there *were several new models on the market now*. She suggested that *one of those could be considered*. *She had asked the manufacturers for information but hadn't yet received any replies*.

Action: Alice to prepare a short report and a decision to be taken at the next meeting.

Exit Test

Over the year, sales of product A have increased sharply. In the first quarter, sales stood at 450 units, but in the last quarter they exceeded 620 units, an increase of more than 70%. *Buyers prefer A because it is a new product and is more up to date than the others*.

Product B's sales, on the other hand, have decreased slightly over the year. At the start of the year, *B's sales* were the same as A's, but they fell to only *a little over 400* by the end of the year. *This is probably because B is an older product and is not as attractive as A. Many buyers are changing from B to A.*

Product C's sales increased in the first and second quarters and reached a peak of about 450. However, they then fell again to below 400 in the last quarter, which is slightly higher than at the start of the year. *Product C is the most expensive of the three products. It is a better product, but too expensive for most people. Sales increased for a time when the price was reduced during a special offer.*

Exit Test: Speaking

Guidelines for the Examiner

The oral test should take about ten minutes. You should give each candidate about five minutes to prepare the two items before starting the test.

A **You will role-play the part of Mr/Mrs Harris, representing *HG Supplies*, a British company which buys equipment for hospitals. Carry out the following steps in your role-play:**

- Greet the candidate and introduce yourself.
- Ask the candidate some general 'small talk' questions.
  Examples:
    'Did you have a good flight?'
    'Have you been to Britain before?'
    'How long will you stay?'
- Tell the candidate that you would like to know something about their company. If necessary, prompt by asking questions about specific points given on the information sheet.
- Ask the candidate if they would like to ask any questions about *HG Supplies*. Use the information below to answer the candidate's questions.

Your company:	*HG Supplies*
Your job title:	Chief Buyer
Company activity:	To buy medical equipment and sell it on to hospitals all over Britain. You buy from abroad and from British companies.
Size of company:	Medium
Employees:	680, mostly buyers, sales representatives who visit hospitals and office administration staff.
Location:	You have regional offices in the North and West of Britain and three warehouses, each one linked to a regional office.

B **Ask the candidate to give their opinions on the qualities of salespeople listed.**

Allow them to speak freely and do not make them more nervous by interrupting too often or being too quick to prompt. If the candidate stops speaking, encourage him or her by asking questions or giving a different opinion to provoke further ideas.
Examples:
    'Why do you say that ...?'
    'Don't you think that ...?'
    'What do you think about ...?'
    'What would you say if ...?'